Dive Into Spanish

CHRIS GREEN

Serf Press

ISBN: 978-0615441818

THIRD EDITION: 2011.

First published in 2004 as "¡Dive In! Spanish: Level 1"

Interior images courtesy of Purdue University.

Printed in the United States of America.

Table of Contents:

Getting Started

Congratulations for choosing to study Spanish! With a little patience and a bit of hard work you'll soon be able to carry on basic conversations with other Spanish–speakers. Before you "dive right in," please read through this section (pay special attention to the pronunciation guide) to give yourself the best start!

A. What this book IS

If you would like to learn basic Spanish on your own, this book is for you. The lessons and activities within this book have been specially designed for the independent learner. Everything you need to learn basic Spanish is contained within this book.

B. What this book IS NOT

This method used in this book is not designed for use as a primary classroom textbook, or for those seeking rapid immersion into the Spanish language.

C. Tips for Success

To learn any language well, you must devote considerable time to studying that language. To excel in this or any language, I recommend studying daily and using spare time throughout your day to review vocabulary words. When you come across new words or concepts that are difficult for you, make note of them in a Spanish notebook so that you will remember to return later and review those rough spots. Don't forget to complete the excercises at the end of each chapter! (Answers are at the back of this book.) It may not be practical for you to study a new lesson every day. Whenever necessary, set aside some days just for review. Don't be concerned with finishing this book within a set time period. Take your time, learn the language well, and *don't forget to have fun!*

D. Pronunciation Guide

Because Spanish pronunciation is entirely different from the English pronunciation that you're used to, take some time and go over this pronunciation guide. Practice saying the words aloud to fix the sounds in your memory. English examples are first, followed by Spanish examples in italics.

Vowels
a – <u>a</u>rt, *casa*
e – <u>e</u>nd, *está*
i – k<u>ey</u>, *fin*
o – <u>o</u>ld, *poco*
u – t<u>u</u>ne, *Lulú*
y – <u>e</u>mu, *y*

> Unlike English, there's only one sound for "O" in Spanish.

Consonants
B – <u>b</u>aby
G – <u>g</u>lue
H – *always* silent
J – the <u>h</u> in <u>h</u>and
Ñ – the <u>ny</u> in Ta<u>ny</u>a
V – sounds like b
Z – an s sound

Combined Letters
LL – the <u>y</u> in <u>y</u>ellow
RR – rolled
QUE – pronounced as **keh**
QUI – pronounced as **kee**

E. Accent Marks

Accent marks are always important features in Spanish words. Leaving them out of words sometimes communicates a different meaning than what you intended. Accent marks always mean that you should stress the vowel and make it more "pronounced" than you normally would. **Tip:** practice saying "**inglés**" to get a feel for accents.

The golden rules for stress and accents are: 1) If the word ends in a **vowel**, **n**, or **s**, the **stress** is placed on the next to last syllable; 2) If the word ends in a **consonant** (other than n or s), the **stress** is on the last syllable; 3) **accents** are used when you want the **stress** to fall on a syllable *other* than where it would naturally fall. **Tip:** practice saying these words aloud: taco, telefono.

F. Wrapping it up

Now that you know a few basics, you're ready to get started! I wish you the best of luck with your new language.

Chris Green

Chapter 1 "¡Hola, amigo!" *(Hello, friend)*

Lesson 1

A. Greeting People

When greeting someone, you generally say "hello" in some form. As with English there are several ways to greet others in Spanish. The list below contains just a few Spanish greetings, several of which you are probably already familiar. Memorize the list below and then continue.

> Use buenos in Buenos Dias, and buenas in Buenas Tardes and Buenas Noches.

Hola – Hello
Buenos días – Good morning
Buenas tardes – Good afternoon
Buenas noches – Good evening

B. How are you?

The easiest way to ask how someone is doing is to say "**¿Qué tal?**" Several common answers are in the list below. You'll learn more later on.

¿Qué tal? – How are you?

Bien – Good
Muy bien – Very good
Mal – Bad
Muy mal – Very bad

If someone asks how you are, and you would like to return the question, you can simply say "**¿y tú?**" (Which literally means "and you?") Additionally, you can thank someone for asking how you are by adding "**gracias**" to your answer. See example 1.

EXAMPLE 1

Spanish:	English:
Pablo: ¡Hola! ¿Qué tal?	Pablo: Hello! How are you?
María: Muy bien, ¿y tú?	María: Very good, and you?
Pablo: ¡Muy bien, gracias!	Pablo: Very good, thanks!

C. What's up?

A common question asked among many young people in the USA and in Spanish–speaking countries when greeting each other is "¿Qué pasa?" or "What's up?" This question can be answered with the words below.

¿Qué pasa? – What's up?

Nada – nothing
No mucho – not much

You can also add "**¿y tú?**" to your answer to return the question.

EXAMPLE 2

Spanish:	English:
Pablo: ¿Qué pasa?	Pablo: What's up?
María: Nada, ¿y tú?	María: Nothing, and you?
Pablo: Nada.	Pablo: Nothing.

D. Saying Goodbye

It's difficult, but sometimes you just have to say goodbye! Several appropriate good–byes are listed below, at least one of which you probably already know.

Adiós – Goodbye
Ciao – Goodbye
Hasta luego – See you later
Hasta pronto – See you soon
Hasta mañana – See you tomorrow

Exercise 1.1

Fill in the blanks to the conversation below using the words you learned in this lesson.

Juan: Buenos _____, Felipe, ¿ Qué _____?

Felipe: Muy bien, gracias, ¿y _____?

Juan: Muy bien.

Felipe: Bien. Ciao.

Juan: ¡Hasta _____!

Lesson 2

A. Identifying People

When speaking to someone in English or Spanish, referring to the individual as "Mr." or "Mrs." shows respect. The words below have the same purpose, and should be used when addressing someone older, someone in authority, or someone you do not know. The words can be abbreviated, as shown in parentheses.

Señor (Sr.) – Mr.
Señora (Sra.) – Mrs.
Señorita (Srta.) – Miss

EXAMPLE 1

Spanish:	English:
Señor Iglesias	Mr. Iglesias
Señora López	Mrs. López
Señorita Verde	Miss Verde

B. Definite/Indefinite Articles

This may look complicated at first, but don't panic! There are exceptions to every rule, but generally, if a word ends with an "o" the word is <u>masculine</u>. If a word ends with an "a" the word is <u>feminine</u>. When used singularly, masculine words have **el** (the) or **un** (a) in front of them. In the same token, singular feminine words have **la** (the) or **una** (a) in front of them. As you've probably picked up, **el** and **la** mean **the** while **un** and **una** mean **a**. **El** and **la** should be used to talk about *specific* objects. **Un** and **una** are used for *non–specific* items. It's important that you understand that a word being masculine or feminine does not necessarily mean that the object that the word represents is masculine or feminine.

<u>Note</u>: Although an "o" or "a" can be indicative of gender at times (think <u>el</u> chic<u>o</u> [the boy] or <u>la</u> chic<u>a</u> [the girl], for example), ordinary objects (food, books, etc.) do not have genders in the biological sense, but do have grammatical genders. For example, it would be absurd to assume that an apple (<u>la</u> manzan<u>a</u>) is feminine in the traditional sense, but grammatically, <u>la</u> manzan<u>a</u> is feminine. Memorize the list and see the example.

un – a (masculine)
una – a (feminine)
el – the (masculine)
la – the (feminine)

EXAMPLE 2

Spanish:	English:
el gato	**the** cat
un gato	**a** cat
la chica	**the** girl
una chica	**a** girl

C. Numbers

In this lesson, you will learn numbers 1–20. Memorize the list below. Take your time memorizing these numbers, as they will be very useful in the next section.

cero – 0
uno – 1
dos – 2
tres – 3
cuatro – 4
cinco – 5
seis – 6
siete – 7
ocho – 8
nueve – 9
diez – 10
once – 11
doce – 12
trece – 13
catorce – 14
quince – 15
dieciséis – 16
diecisiete – 17
dieciocho – 18
diecinueve – 19
veinte – 20

Exercise 1.2

Insert the correct direct or indirect article in front of the words below.

_____ carro (the car).

_____ taco (a taco).

_____ tienda (the store).

_____ maleta (a suitcase).

_____ manzana (the apple).

<u>Lesson 3</u>

A. Days of the Week

The Spanish days of the week are listed below. Unlike English, days of the week and months of the year are not capitalized. Practice saying these out loud and memorize them before continuing.

lunes – Monday
martes – Tuesday
miércoles – Wednesday
jueves – Thursday
viernes – Friday
sábado – Saturday
domingo – Sunday

B. Months

On the next page you will find the twelve months of the year. You won't have much trouble memorizing these, as most of them are very similar to their English equivalents.

enero – January
febrero – February
marzo – March
abril – April
mayo – May
junio – June
julio – July
agosto – August
septiembre – September
octubre – October
noviembre – November
diciembre – December

C. Numbers

Now it's time to learn numbers 21–29. These nine numbers are formed by changing the second "e" in veinte to an "i" and adding the appropriate number from one to 9. The complete list is below. If you can remember how to form these numbers, memorization won't be necessary.

veintiuno – 21
veintidós – 22
veintitrés – 23
veinticuatro – 24
veinticinco – 25
veintiséis – 26
veintisiete – 27
veintiocho – 28
veintinueve – 29

Exercise 1.3

Form the numbers below using what you learned in this lesson.

Twenty–one _____.

Veintinueve _____.

Twenty–two _____.

Veintiocho _____.

Twenty–five _____.

Veintitrés _____.

Chapter 2 "Preguntas" *(Questions)*

Lesson 1

A. Ser

It's time to learn your first Spanish verb. Ser means "to be." This verb is used to express several things. With ser, you can tell others what your name is, what you are like, and where you are from. In the left column are the first three conjugations (or, in other words, different verb forms) of ser (in bold) and the pronouns I, you (familiar), he, she, and you (formal). The right column contains the English translations.

EXAMPLE 1

Spanish:	English:
Yo **soy**	I **am**
Tú **eres**	You **are**
Él/Ella/Usted **es**	He/She **is**/You **are**

> Tú is for friends! Ud. is for your boss or teacher.

B. What is usted (Ud.)?

Usted (abbreviated **Ud.**) is a formal way of saying "**you.**" Usted shows respect, and should be used when speaking to someone you do not know, or someone who is older. Use the tú form when talking to friends.

C. I am...

As you already know, ser can be used to express several things. Right now, you're going to learn how to tell someone who "I am," who "you are," and who "she is." (To say who "he is," just replace **ella** with **él**.) See the example.

EXAMPLE 2

Spanish:	English:
Yo soy Pablo.	**I am** Pablo.
Tú eres Amelia.	**You are** Amelia
Ella es Sandra.	**She is** Sandra.

Exercise 2.1

Fill in the blanks below.

Yo _____ Elena.

Ella _____ una chica.

Él _____ Roberto.

Tú _____ Maricarmen.

Chapter 2

Lesson 2

A. Question Words

We ask lots of questions every day. What time is it? Who are you? Where is the restaurant? It's important to be able to ask questions like these in Spanish, especially if you plan on visiting a place where Spanish is spoken. Below are several question words that you can use to ask different types of questions in Spanish. Take some time to memorize this list. These words will be very important for the following lessons.

In questions, Use a question mark ? plus an inverted one ¿ at the beginning.

¿Qué? – What
¿Quién? – Who
¿Dónde? – Where
¿Cómo? – How
¿Cuánto? – How much

B. Who are you?

As you already know, you can tell someone your name by saying "**Yo soy** _____." But how do you ask for someone's name? See the question and answer below and then continue to the example on the next page.

¿Quién eres? – Who are you?
Yo soy _____. – I am _____.

Mucho gusto – Pleased to meet you
El gusto es mío – The pleasure is mine

EXAMPLE 1

Spanish:	English:
Carlos: ¿Quién eres?	Carlos: Who are you?
Quico: Yo soy Quico.	Quico: I am Quico.
Carlos: Mucho gusto, Quico.	Carlos: Pleased to meet you, Quico.

C. Who is he/she?

Asking who "**he is**" or who "**she is**" is just as simple! This can also be used to ask who "**you** (formal) **are**." Just replace **él** or **ella** with **usted**.

> Remember: el means the while él (accent) means he.

¿Quién es él/ella? – Who is he/she?
Él/ella es _____. – He/she is _____.

¿Quién es Ud.? – Who are you?
Ud. es _____. – You are _____.

EXAMPLE 2

Spanish:	English:
María: ¿Quién es ella?	María: Who is she?
Enrique: Ella es Carmen.	Enrique: She is Carmen.

Exercise 2.2 #1

Marta: Hola, ¿_____ eres?

Carlos: _____ Carlos.

Marta: Hola, Carlos. Mucho _____.

Carlos: El _____ es _____. ¿Quién es ella?

Marta: Ella _____ Maricarmen.

Carlos: Hola, Maricarmen. ¡_____ gusto!

Exercise 2.2 #2

Marcos: Hola, ¿Quién _____ Ud.?

María: Yo _____ María. ¿y Quién es _____?

Marcos: _____ soy Marcos. ¡Mucho _____!

18

Lesson 3

A. Describing Yourself

To describe yourself you can also use "**Yo soy** _____." You can describe yourself (and others) with any of the adjectives below.

inteligente – intelligent
estúpido – stupid
moreno – dark (hair/complexion)
rubio – blond
alto – tall
bajo – short
simpático – nice
antipático – not nice
serio – serious
divertido – fun

B. What are you like?

As seen in the example below, you can include multiple adjectives to describe yourself by using commas and **y** (and). The gender of adjectives should generally be adjusted to fit the gender of the nouns they modify. You are a noun, so therefore if you are describing yourself and you are male, any adjectives that describe you should end in "**o**." If you are female, any adjectives that describe you should end in "**a**."

Note: Words that end in "**e**" such as **inteligente** are not gender specific, and do not require this adjustment. See the example on the next page.

¿Cómo eres? – What are you like?
Yo soy _____. – I am _____.

EXAMPLE 1

Spanish:	English:
Juan: ¿Cómo eres?	Juan: What are you like?
Pedro: Yo soy inteligente y bajo.	Pedro: I am intelligent and short.

C. What is he/she like?

In this section you will learn how to ask what he or she is like. Again, remember to make your adjectives gender–specific.

¿**Cómo es él/ella?** – What is he/she like?
Él/ella es _____. – He/she is _____.

EXAMPLE 2

Spanish:	English:
María: ¿Cómo es ella?	María: What is she like?
Antonio: Ella es simpática y rubia.	Antonio: She is nice and blond.

D. Where are you from?

Telling someone where you are from is similar to the first two sections of this lesson, with only one additional word. Just say "**Yo soy de** _____." to tell someone where you are from. See the example on the next page.

¿**De dónde eres?** – Where are you from?
Yo soy de _____. – I am from _____.

EXAMPLE 3

Spanish:	English:
Juan: ¿De dónde eres?	Juan: Where are you from?
Pedro: Yo soy de los Estados Unidos	Pedro: I am from the United States.

E. Where is he/she from?

Asking "**Where is he or she from?**" is similar to the previous question. Just change "eres" to "es" and add "él," "ella," or "usted." See the example below.

¿**De dónde es él/ella?** – Where is he/she from?
Él/Ella es de _____. – He/she is from _____.

EXAMPLE 4

Spanish:	English:
Juan: ¿De dónde es él?	Juan: Where is he from?
Pedro: Él es de Cuba.	Pedro: He is from Cuba.

Exercise 2.3

Fill in the missing information below.

1) ¿Cómo eres?

Yo soy _____.

2) ¿_____ dónde eres?

Yo _____ de los Estados Unidos.

3) ¿De dónde _____ él?

_____ es de España.

4) ¿Cómo es _____?

Ella es _____ (blonde) y _____ (nice).

5) ¿Eres _____?

Sí, yo _____ morena.

Chapter 3 "Más preguntas" *(More questions)*

Lesson 1

A. More Ser

You learned the first three conjugations (verb forms) of the verb <u>ser</u> in the previous chapter. There are two more you will now learn. In the left column you will find the two new conjugations with the pronouns we, they (masculine), they (feminine), and you (formal/plural). The right column contains the English translations. See the example.

EXAMPLE 1

Spanish	English
Nosotros **somos**	We **are**
Ellos/Ellas/Uds. **son**	They **are**

B. What is ustedes (Uds.)?

Ustedes (abbreviated **Uds.**), the plural form of **Usted**, loosely means **"you all."** **Uds.** should be used when speaking to more than one person. For example: "Do you all want to join me for dinner?" is a situation when you should use the **ustedes** (Uds.) form. The pronoun ustedes is not always included with the verb conjugations in this book – just remember that you can still use this instead of ellos or ellas. See the example on the next page.

C. We Are

Now you're going to use the conjugations of <u>ser</u> you learned on the previous page to tell someone who **"we are,"** and who **"they are."** For now, most of the nouns and adjectives you have learned can be made plural by simply adding an "s." Don't forget to adjust the genders of adjectives to reflect the genders of nouns.

EXAMPLE 2

Spanish	English
Nosotros somos chicos.	**We are** boys.
Ellas son americanas.	**They are** Americans.
Ellos son estudiantes.	**They are** students.

D. More Definite/Indefinite Articles

Now that you have a handle on <u>singular</u> definite and indefinite articles, it's time to learn the plural forms. The articles for plural masculine words are **unos** and **los**. **Unos** is the plural form of **un**, and is therefore used for *non–specific* items. **Los** is the plural of **el**, which makes it useful when referring to *specific* items. As you might have expected, **unas** is the feminine plural form of **una**, and is used for – you guessed it – multiple non–specific items. Lastly, **las** is the feminine plural form of **la** and is used for specific items.

unos – some (plural, masculine)
unas – some (plural, feminine)
los – the (plural, masculine)
las – the (plural, feminine)

EXAMPLE 3

Spanish:	English:
los perros	**the** dogs
unos perros	**some** dogs
las chicas	**the** girls
unas chicas	**some** girls

Exercise 3.1

Insert the correct article in front of the words below.

_____ bolígrafos (the pens).

_____ libros (some books).

_____ escuelas (some schools).

_____ casas (the houses).

_____ papas (some potatoes).

Chapter 3

Lesson 2

A. Who are you all?

In the last lesson, you learned to say who "**we are**" and who "**they are**." When you meet a group of new people, here is how you can ask who "**you all are.**"

¿Quiénes son Uds.? – Who are you all?
Nosotros somos _____. – We are _____.

EXAMPLE 1

Spanish	English
<u>Alfredo:</u> ¿Quiénes son Uds.?	<u>Alfredo:</u> Who are you all?
<u>Los chicos:</u> Nosotros somos estudiantes.	<u>The boys:</u> We are students.

B. Who are they?

Asking who "they are," is very similar. Remember to use **ellos** for males and **ellas** for females. For a mixed group of people, use **ellos**.

¿Quiénes son ellos/ellas? – Who are they?
Ellos/ellas son _____. – They are _____.

EXAMPLE 2

Spanish	English
<u>Mateo:</u> ¿Quiénes son ellas?	<u>Mateo:</u> Who are they?
<u>Elena:</u> Ellas son profesoras.	<u>Elena:</u> They are teachers.

C. What are we like?

You can tell someone what "**we are**" like by saying "**Nosotros somos _____.**" Remember that adjectives from the previous chapter can be used with the addition of "**s**" to the ends to make them plural. Don't forget to adjust the gender of adjectives to match the gender the noun! See the example.

¿Cómo son Uds.? – What are you all like?
Nosotros somos _____. – We are _____.

EXAMPLE 3

Spanish	English
<u>Josefina:</u> ¿Cómo son Uds.?	<u>Josefina:</u> What are you all like?
<u>Cecilia y Jorge:</u> Nosotros somos inteligentes y altos.	<u>Cecilia and Jorge:</u> We are intelligent and tall.

D. What are they like?

Below, you will learn to ask what "**they are**" like. Remember to change **ellos** or **ellas** to reflect the gender of the people you are asking about. See the example.

¿Cómo son ellos/ellas? – What are they like?
Ellos/ellas son _____. – They are _____.

EXAMPLE 4

Spanish	English
<u>Eduardo:</u> ¿Cómo son ellas?	<u>Eduardo:</u> What are they like?
<u>Diego:</u> Ellas son simpáticas.	<u>Diego:</u> They are nice.

E. Where are we from?

To tell where "**we are**" from, say "**Nosotros somos de _____.**" Fill in the blank with a country, town, state, etc. Try all three if you feel adventurous! See the example.

¿De dónde son Uds.? – Where are you all from?
Nosotros somos de _____. – We are from _____.

EXAMPLE 5

Spanish	English
Daniela: ¿De dónde son Uds.?	Eduardo: Where are you all from?
Susana y Felipe: Nosotros somos de Chile.	Susana and Felipe: We are from Chile.

F. Where are they from?

Now we will ask where "they are" from. Don't forget to use **ellos** or **ellas** accordingly. See the example.

¿De dónde son ellos/ellas? – Where are they from?
Ellos/ellas son de _____. – They are from _____.

EXAMPLE 6

Spanish	English
Roberto: ¿De dónde son ellos?	Roberto: Where are they from?
Nora: Ellos son de Puerto Rico.	Nora: They are from Puerto Rico.

Lesson 3

A. More Numbers

It's time to learn numbers 30 through 100. Don't panic! You only have to learn **8** new numbers. How's that? Numbers 1–9 that you learned a few days ago can be added to the end of the numbers you will learn today. Memorize the list below before continuing.

treinta – 30
cuarenta – 40
cincuenta – 50
sesenta – 60
setenta – 70
ochenta – 80
noventa – 90
cien(to) – 100

To form a number like 31, for example, start with **treinta**, add **y**, and then add **uno**. You end up with **treinta y uno** (which is literally "thirty and one"). That's all there is to it! See the example below.

EXAMPLE 1

Spanish:	English:
Cuarenta y cinco	Forty–five
Noventa y ocho	Ninety–eight
Veintinueve	Twenty–nine

B. What time is it?

"**What time is it?**" is a question we ask often. There are two answers for this question in Spanish. The first answer below is "**Es la _____.**" which should be used when it is **1:00** to **1:30**. Otherwise, for **2:00** to **12:30**, use the second answer "**Son las _____.**" To say how many minutes past the hour it is, just add "**y**" between the hour and minutes.

¿Qué hora es? – What time is it?
Es la _____. – It is _____.
Son las _____. – It is _____.

The phrases below can be attached onto the end of your answer to tell the time of day.

de la mañana – In the morning (A.M.)
de la tarde – In the afternoon (P.M.)
de la noche – At night (P.M.)

The following phrases can be used to more easily tell what time it is. Use **menos** to say how many minutes until the next hour it is. In Spanish, to say "15 til 2" you would literally say, "2 minus 14" or "Son las dos menos catorce." Use **media** when telling someone it's 30 minutes past the hour. For example: "Son las cinco y media," or "It's 5:30." **Cuarto** is similar. Use it when telling someone it is 15 minutes past the hour or 15 minutes until the next hour. "Quarter past three" becomes "Son las tres y cuarto," and "quarter til 7" becomes "Son las siete menos cuarto."

> For telling time, use fifteen and cuarto interchangeably.

menos – minus
media – half
cuarto – quarter

EXAMPLE 2

Spanish	English
Dolores: ¿Qué hora es?	Dolores: What time is it?
Arturo: Son las dos y quince de la tarde.	Arturo: It is two fifteen in the afternoon.

C. What day is it?

When you visit a Spanish speaking country, you may need to ask what day it is because of the time difference. Be sure you know the days of the week before you continue. See the example below.

¿Qué día es hoy? – What is today?
Hoy es _____. – Today is _____.

EXAMPLE 3

Spanish	English
Ernesto: ¿Qué día es hoy?	Ernesto: What is today?
Fredrico: Hoy es martes.	Fredrico: Today is Tuesday.

D. What is today's date?

It's easy to lose track of time when you're vacationing in a Spanish country. To ask someone for today's date, simply use the question below, or go a bit further and add the month!

¿Qué fecha es hoy? – What is today's date?
Hoy es _____. – Today is _____.
Hoy es el __ de ____. – Today is the (day) of (month).

Exercise 3.3 #1

Form the numbers below.

Forty–three _____.

Sixty–seven _____.

Fifty–one _____.

Eighty–two _____.

Twenty–five _____.

One hundred thirty–one _____.

Exercise 3.3 #2

Practice forming times and dates below.

1) May 6

_____

2) 3:30 P.M.

_____

3) June 5

_____

4) 5:15 A.M.

_____

Chapter 4 – "Estar" *(To be)*

Lesson 1

A. Estar

Now that you've mastered <u>ser</u>, it's time to learn another verb: <u>estar</u>. <u>Estar</u> means **"to be."** Yes, <u>ser</u> also means **"to be."** How's that? For starters, <u>ser</u> describes characteristics that are *usually* <u>permanent</u>, while <u>estar</u> describes conditions that are *usually* <u>temporary</u>. In general, <u>ser</u> refers to who you are and where you're from. These are things that will not change. <u>Estar</u> is used to tell where you are and how you feel. These are conditions that change. Below are the five conjugations of <u>estar</u> (with pronouns to the left). Take time to memorize these; then continue.

EXAMPLE 1

Spanish	English
Yo **estoy**	I **am**
Tú **estás**	You **are**
Él, Ella, Ud. **está**	He/she **is**
Nosotros **estamos**	We **are**
Ellos, Ellas, Uds. **están**	They **are**

Don't forget to use Ud. instead of Tú, formally and Uds. to address groups

Chapter 4

Lesson 2

A. Where I Am

To tell someone where "**I am**", say "**Yo estoy en _____.**" As you know by now, saying where "**you are**," where "**he is**," where "**she is**," where "**we are**," and where "**they are**," will follow the same pattern. Just take the pronoun and conjugation and add "**en**," to the end to tell where someone is. See the example.

Yo estoy en _____. – I am in _____.
Él/Ella está en _____. – He/she is in _____.
Nosotros estamos en _____. – We are in _____.

EXAMPLE 1

Spanish	English
Yo estoy en los Estados Unidos.	I am in the United States.
Ella está en Cuba.	She is in Cuba.
Nosotros estamos en la escuela.	We are in school.

B. Asking Where Someone Is

To ask where someone is, use the question word **¿dónde?**. You should be just about ready to start forming your own questions! But for now, see the list on the next page to ask where different people are. See the example on the next page.

1) **¿Dónde estás?** – Where are you?
A) **Yo estoy en _____.** – I am in _____.

2) **¿Dónde está él/ella?** – Where is he/she?
A) **Él/ella está en _____.** – He/she is in _____.

3) **¿Dónde están ellos/ellas?**
– Where are they?

A) **Ellos/Ellas están en _____.**

33

– They are in _____.

4) ¿Dónde están Uds.?
– Where are you all?

A) Nosotros están en _____.
– We are in _____.

C. Places

The list below includes a few words that you can use with estar to say where you and others are. Just insert any one of these nouns into the blanks in the questions and answers above. See the example.

el restaurante – restaurant
la biblioteca – library
el museo – museum
el parque – park
la escuela – school
la tienda – store
el cine – movie theater

EXAMPLE 2

Spanish	English
Raul: Yo estoy en el museo. ¿Dónde estás?	Raul: I am in the museum. Where are you?
Daniela: Yo estoy en la tienda.	Daniela: I am in the store.

Exercise 4.2

Fill in the blanks to the conversation below using the words you learned in this lesson.

Raul: Hola, Daniela. ¿Dónde está Maricarmen?

Daniela: Maricarmen _____ en la biblioteca.

Raul: Ah. ¿_____ están los estudiantes?

Daniela: Jajaja! Los estudiantes _____ en la escuela.

34

Chapter 4

Lesson 3

A. How I Feel

You already know that you can ask someone how they are by saying "**¿Qué tal?**" You can ask that same question by using <u>estar</u>. With <u>estar</u>, however, you can ask more than one person how they feel and ask how a third person feels. The adjectives you learned in the first chapter are included here for reference, in addition to a few new ones. See the questions and example below.

bien – good
mal – bad
muy bien – very good
muy mal – very bad
enfermo(a) – sick
aburrido(a) – bored
nervioso(a) – nervous
triste – sad

¿Cómo estás? – How are you?

¿Cómo está él/ella? – How is he/she?

¿Cómo están ellos/ellas/Uds.? – How are they/you all?

EXAMPLE 1

Spanish	English
<u>Emilia</u>: ¿Cómo está ella?	<u>Emilia</u>: How is she?
<u>Pablo</u>: Muy mal. ¿Cómo están Uds.?	<u>Pablo</u>: Very bad. How are you all?
<u>Emilia</u>: Bien, gracias.	<u>Emilia</u>: Good, thanks.

¡Yo estoy *muy* bien!

Exercise 4.3

Fill in the blanks to the conversation below using the words you learned in this lesson.

Emilia: Hola, Pablo. ¿_____ estás?

Pablo: Estoy _____, ¿y tú?

Emilia: Bien, _____.

Pablo: ¿Y Marco? ¿Cómo _____ él?

Emilia: Él _____ bien.

Chapter 5 – "Ir" *(To go)*

Lesson 1

A. Ir

It's time to learn another verb. <u>Ir</u> means "**to go**" and is always followed by an "**a**." This can be used to express where you are going, how you are going there, or something you are going to do in the future. Below are the five conjugations of the verb <u>ir</u>. Memorize these before continuing. See the example.

Yo **voy**
Tú **vas**
Él, Ella, Ud. **va**
Nosotros **vamos**
Ellos, Ellas, Uds. **van**

EXAMPLE 1

Spanish	English
Yo **voy**	I **go**
Tú **vas**	You **go**
Él, Ella, Ud. **va**	He/she **goes**
Nosotros **vamos**	We **go**
Ellos, Ellas, Uds. **van**	They **go**

B. I Am Going To

Below you will learn to tell others where you are going. The nouns you learned in 4.2 (el museo, la biblioteca, etc.) can also be used with ir in the sentences below. See the example.

Yo voy a _____. – I am going to _____.

As you have probably already figured out, you can use the rest of the conjugations of ir the same way we just used the **yo** form.

Tú vas a _____. – You are going to _____.

Él/Ella va a _____. – He/she is going to _____.
Nosotros vamos a _____. – We are going to _____.
Ellos/Ellas van a _____. – They are going to _____.

EXAMPLE 2

Spanish	English
Yo voy a la tienda.	I am going to the store.
Yo voy a la biblioteca.	I am going to the library.

C. Where Are We Going?

The question word ¿Dónde? (A is added to the front of Dónde, instead of after the verb) should be used to ask where someone is going.

¿Adónde vas? – Where are you going?
¿Adónde va él/ella? – Where is he/she going?
¿Adónde van ellos/ellas? – Where are they going?

EXAMPLE 3

Spanish	English
<u>Marcos:</u> Voy a la escuela. ¿A dónde vas?	<u>Marcos:</u> I am going to school. Where are you going?
<u>Jose:</u> ¡Voy a la escuela, también!	<u>Jose:</u> I am going to school, too!

Chapter 5

<u>Lesson 2</u>

A. Contractions

In this lesson you will learn a few contractions. See the example after studying the explanations below.

<u>A + EL = AL</u>

As you know, **ir** will always be followed by an "**a**." If you want to say "**I am going to the restaurant,**" it is difficult (and incorrect) to say "Voy a ir a el restaurante." So, combine **a** and **el**, to form **al**. Now the sentence reads, "**Voy a ir al restaurante.**" Doesn't that flow much more smoothly?

<u>DE + EL = DEL</u>

You will not use "**de**" with the verb ir, but you will need this contraction later. **De** (of/from) is most commonly used with the verb **ser**. As you know, you tell someone where you are from by saying, "**Yo soy de** _____." Let's use "**el Brasil,**" as the example. It's difficult (and incorrect) to say "**Yo soy de el Brasil.**" Just combine the **de** and **el** to form **del**. The new sentence says, "**Yo soy del Brasil.**"

<u>Antes De and Despues De</u>

Antes de means "before" while **después de** means "after." You can use these to tell when an event happens. Let's use school as an example, "**Después de la escuela, voy a la tienda.**" (After school, I go to the store.) That's it! Simple, right? Use **antes de**, exactly the same way. "**Antes de la escuela voy a su casa.**" (Before school, I go to your house.)

EXAMPLE 1

Spanish	English
Yo voy a ir **al** restaurante.	I am going to go to the restaurant.
Yo soy **del** Brasil.	I am from Brazil.
Después de la escuela voy a la tienda.	**After** school I go to the store.
Antes de la escuela voy a su casa.	**Before** school I go to your house.

Exercise 5.2

Fill in the blanks to the conversation below using the correct contractions.

Ella va a ir _____ banco.

Nosotros somos _____ Brazil.

Yo voy ____ _____ escuela.

Elena _____ a _____ tienda.

Tú eres _____ los Estados Unidos.

Chapter 5

Lesson 3

A. How To Get Around

Below are a few common ways of traveling. To tell someone how you are traveling, use the appropriate conjugation of <u>ir</u> followed by "**por**" and then how you are traveling. The only exception is when using "a pie." See the example.

auto – Car
bicicleta – Bicycle
a pie – On Foot (walking)
metro – Metro/Subway
autobús – Bus

EXAMPLE 1

Spanish	English
Voy por carro.	I am going by car.
Vamos por bicicleta	We are going by bicycle
Van a pie.	They are going by foot.

B. What Are You Going to Do?

Ir can be used to express what you are going to do. "I am going to study," or "I am going to eat," for example. Constructing these sentences is simple, just use the appropriate conjugation of ir, then add "a" then add an infinitive verb from the list on the next page. Because you are using these verbs with ir, you do not have to conjugate them. Also note that you can use ir as the second verb and leave it in the infinitive form to say "I am going to go to _____." See the example.

Ir + a + infinitive verb

comer – to eat
estudiar – to study
dormir – to sleep
nadar – to swim
conducir – to drive
hablar – to talk

41

EXAMPLE 2

Spanish	English
Voy a comer.	I am going to eat.
Vamos a nadar.	We are going to swim.
Ella va a conducir.	She is going to drive.
Voy a ir a la tienda.	I am going to go to the store.

Exercise 5.3

Fill in the blanks to the conversation below using what you have learned in this lesson.

Vamos _____ el carro.

Voy _____ pie.

Voy a _____ (swim).

Ella va a _____ a la biblioteca.

Chapter 6 – "Muchos Verbos" *(Many Verbs)*

Lesson 1

A. –ar Verbs

Now you know three verbs – ser, ir and estar. It's time to learn a few more! The three verbs you already know are **irregular** verbs. What this means is that those verbs are harder to conjugate. The good news is that all of the verbs you will learn in this lesson are **regular** verbs. Each regular verb has a stem (root word) which does not change, and uses a standard set of endings. So as long as you know the standard set of endings, you can conjugate any regular verb!

B. How to Conjugate a Regular –ar Verb

Regular verbs are very easy to conjugate! We'll practice with the verb **hablar**, which means "**to talk**." First remove the **–ar** ending. You now have **habl-**. Then, just add an ending. There are five endings for regular **–ar** verbs. These are listed below.

–o – I.
–as – You.
–a – He/she/you (formal).
–amos – We.
–an – They/you all (formal).

Let's say, "**I talk**." Look at the endings above. You see that the correct ending is **–o**. Add it to the end, and you now have **hablo**. It's as simple as that! This method works for all the verbs listed on the next page.

C. New Verbs To Learn

Below are five new verbs for you to memorize. Also be sure you memorize the five endings above. Remember that because these verbs are regular, you can conjugate them like any –ar verb. (A cheat sheet, including all the conjugations of these verbs, is on this page and the next. The stems, or root words, are underlined.)

llegar – to arrive
tomar – to take
nadar – to swim

mirar – to look at
hablar – to speak

llegar:

Spanish	English
Yo **llego**	I **arrive**
Tú **llegas**	You **arrive**
Él, Ella **llega**	He/she **arrives**
Nosotros **llegamos**	We **arrive**
Ellos, Ellas **llegan**	They **arrive**

tomar:

Spanish	English
Yo **tomo**	I **take**
Tú **tomas**	You **take**
Él, Ella **toma**	He/she **takes**
Nosotros **tomamos**	We **take**
Ellos, Ellas **toman**	They **take**

nadar:

Spanish	English
Yo **nado**	I **swim**
Tú **nadas**	You **swim**
Él, Ella **nada**	He/she **swim**
Nosotros **nadamos**	We **swim**
Ellos, Ellas **nadan**	They **swim**

mirar:

Spanish	English
Yo **miro**	I **look**
Tú **miras**	You **look**
Él, Ella **mira**	He/she **look**
Nosotros **miramos**	We **look**
Ellos, Ellas **miran**	They **look**

hablar:

Spanish	English
Yo **hablo**	I **speak**
Tú **hablas**	You **speak**
Él, Ella **habla**	He/she **speaks**
Nosotros **hablamos**	We **speak**
Ellos, Ellas **hablan**	They **speak**

D. Hablar

Hablar, which means "to speak," can be used to ask someone what language he or she speaks. Just say "¿Hablas _____?"

¿**Hablas** _____? – Do you speak _____?

inglés – English
alemán – German
francés – French
español – Spanish

Languages are never capitalized in Spanish.

EXAMPLE 1

Spanish	English
Carmen: ¿Hablas alemán?	Carmen: Do you speak German?
Pablo: Sí, hablo alemán. ¿y tú?	Pablo: Yes, I speak German. And you?
Carmen: No, no hablo alemán.	Carmen: No, I don't speak German.

E. Mirar

Mirar means "to look at." You will probably use this verb most often to express "watching TV." See the nouns below, and then proceed to the example.

la televisión – television
los deportes – sports

45

EXAMPLE 2

Spanish	English
María: ¿Qué miras?	María: What do you watch?
Sr. Verde: Miro los deportes. ¿y tú?	Sr. Verde: I watch sports. And you?
María: Miro los deportes, también.	María: I watch sports, too.

Exercise 6.1

Fill in the blanks below using the words you learned in this lesson.

- ¿_____ miras?

- _____ los deportes, ¿y tú?

- Miro _____, también.

- Hablas inglés?

- No, no hablo _____. _____ español y alemán.

Chapter 6

Lesson 2

A. More Regular –AR verbs

In this lesson you will learn four more regular –ar verbs. These verbs can be conjugated just like the verbs you learned yesterday! Remove the –ar, and add the correct ending. If you need to review those endings again, look over Lesson 1 now. Below are the four new verbs. Memorize them and practice conjugating them! All of these verbs are conjugated on the next page.

necesitar – to need
comprar – to buy
tocar – to play (music)
trabajar – to work

necesitar:

Spanish	English
Yo **necesito**	I **need**
Tú **necesitas**	You **need**
Él, Ella **necesita**	He/she **needs**
Nosotros **necesitamos**	We **need**
Ellos, Ellas **necesitan**	They **need**

comprar:

Spanish	English
Yo **compro**	I **buy**
Tú **compras**	You **buy**
Él, Ella **compra**	He/she **buys**
Nosotros **compramos**	We **buy**
Ellos, Ellas **compran**	They **buy**

tocar:

Spanish	English
Yo **toco**	I **play**
Tú **tocas**	You **play**
Él, Ella **toca**	He/she **plays**
Nosotros **tocamos**	We **play**
Ellos, Ellas **tocan**	They **play**

trabajar:

Spanish	English
Yo **trabajo**	I **work**
Tú **trabajas**	You **work**
Él, Ella **trabaja**	He/she **works**
Nosotros **trabajamos**	We **work**
Ellos, Ellas **trabajan**	They **work**

B. Things I Need

If you visit a Spanish–speaking country, you'll probably forget to pack something! Use necesitar to ask for items that you need. You can use the words below with comprar, as well! Remember from lesson 1.2 that you must change el to un, or la to una to ask for a specific item (**the** glass of water sitting in front of you) or a nonspecific item (**a** glass of water).

Necesito _____. – I need _____.

El boleto – ticket
La medicina – medicine
La toalla – towel
La estampilla – stamp
El jabón – soap
El vaso con agua – glass of water

EXAMPLE 1

Spanish	English
Diego: Necesito una estampilla, por favor.	Diego: I need a stamp, please
Sandra: No es problema.	Sandra: No problem.
Diego: Gracias.	Diego: Thank you.

C. Trabajar, Tocar

A few vocabulary words for use with these verbs are below. Practice forming sentences with these verbs and nouns.

Toco _____. – I play _____.

el piano – piano
la guitarra – guitar

Trabajo en _____. – I work in _____.

el restaurante – the restaurant
la tienda – the store
la oficina – the office
a veces – sometimes
todos los días – every day

EXAMPLE 2

Spanish	English
Maricarmen: ¿Qué tocas?	Maricarmen: What do you play?
Emilia: Toco la guitarra. ¿Dónde trabajas?	Emilia: I play the guitar. Where do you work?
Maricarmen: Trabajo en una tienda.	Maricarmen: I work in a a store.
Emilia: ¿Trabajas todos los días o a veces?	Emilia: Do you work every day, or just sometimes?
Maricarmen: Trabajo todos los días.	Maricarmen: I work every day.

Exercise 6.2

Fill in the blanks below using the words you learned in this lesson.

- ¿_____ necesitas?

- _____ una estampilla.

- ¿_____ trabajas?

- _____ en un restaurante.

Chapter 6

<u>Lesson 3</u>

A. Affirmative and Negative

You now know how to tell people who you are, where you work, and what you do. It's time to learn how to tell people who you aren't, and what you don't do. In a word, it's time to learn how to say **no**. When asked a question, you can respond with sí or no. If you respond with sí, just add sí to the front of your answer. If you say no, however, you must say no twice to make the verb negative. The first no means simply "no," while the second no means "don't." Finally, "también" means "also" or "as well," and can be added to an affirmative answer.

Affirmative:
¿Nadas mucho? – Do you swim often?
<u>Sí</u>, nado mucho. – <u>Yes</u>, I swim often.

Nado mucho, también. – I swim often, <u>as well</u>.

Negative:
¿Nadas mucho? – Do you swim often?
<u>No, no</u> nado mucho. – <u>No</u>, I <u>don't</u> swim often.

EXAMPLE 1

Spanish	English
No, no nado.	**No**, I **don't** swim.
Ella **no** habla.	She **does not** talk.
Sí, miro la television.	**Yes**, I watch tv.

¡Sí, como el chocolate!

Chapter 7 – "Más Verbos" *(More Verbs)*

Lesson 1

A. Regular –er, –ir Verbs

This lesson will add five more verbs to your vocabulary. Today you will learn to conjugate –er and –ir verbs. Just like regular –ar verbs, regular –er and –ir verbs have an unchanging stem and follow a standard set of endings. –er and –ir verbs have practically the same endings. In fact, the only difference between the two sets of endings lies in the **nosotros** form. First we'll start with –er verbs. Memorize the endings below.

–o – I
–es – you
–e – he/she/Ud.
–emos – we
–en – they/Uds.

B. Three –er Verbs

Below are three new –er verbs for you to memorize. These can be conjugated by removing the –er and adding the appropriate ending above. These verbs are conjugated for you on the next page. (Again, the stems are underlined)

beber – to drink
comer – to eat
leer – to read

beber:

Spanish	English
Yo **bebo**	I **drink**
Tú **bebes**	You **drink**
Él, Ella **bebe**	He/she **drinks**
Nosotros **bebemos**	We **drink**
Ellos, Ellas **beben**	They **drink**

comer:

Spanish	English
Yo **como**	I **eat**
Tú **comes**	You **eat**
Él, Ella **come**	He/she **eats**
Nosotros **comemos**	We **eat**
Ellos, Ellas **comen**	They **eat**

leer:

Spanish	English
Yo **leo**	I **read**
Tú **lees**	You **read**
Él, Ella **lee**	He/she **reads**
Nosotros **leemos**	We **read**
Ellos, Ellas **leen**	They **read**

C. Food and Drink

Below are a few words you can use with the verbs comer and beber.

el agua – water
la leche – milk
el café – coffee

el pan – bread
unos huevos – eggs
una ensalada – salad

Even though agua ends with an 'a,' it's a masculine word. Use 'el.'

EXAMPLE 3

Spanish	English
Marcos: ¿Qué comes?	Marcos: What are you eating?
Jose: Como una ensalada.	Jose: I'm eating a salad.

D. –ir Verbs

–ir verbs are conjugated just like –er verbs, with the exception of the **Nosotros** form. Instead of using, "**–emos,**" you will use, "**–imos.**" See the list of endings for regular –ir verbs below.

–o – I
–es – you
–e – he/she
–imos – we
–en – they

E. Two –ir Verbs

Below are two new –ir verbs for you to memorize. Remember, these can be conjugated just like –er verbs with the exception of the **Nosotros** form. Refer back to the endings above if needed. As always, the verbs are fully conjugated on this page and the next.

vivir – to live
escribir – to write

vivir:

Spanish	English
Yo **vivo**	I **live**
Tú **vives**	You **live**
Él, Ella **vive**	He/she **lives**
Nosotros **vivimos**	We **live**
Ellos, Ellas **viven**	They **live**

escribir:

Spanish	English
Yo **escribo**	I **write**
Tú **escribes**	You **write**
Él, Ella **escribe**	He/she **writes**
Nosotros **escribimos**	We **write**
Ellos, Ellas **escriben**	They **write**

Chapter 7

Lesson 2

A. Irregular –er, –ir Verbs

In this lesson you will learn five irregular –er and –ir verbs. Remember that the stems of irregular verbs change and do not follow the standard set of endings for –er and –ir verbs. Because of this, you must memorize each verb conjugation. The verbs in this section particularly will be used later in the book, so practice using them now.

B. More –er Verbs

Below are one new irregular verb and two regular verbs that are similar to irregular verbs. Tener is irregular, but querer and poder are regular. Querer and poder have stem changes, which makes them "seem" irregular. (In querer, the first "e" changes to "ie," and in poder the "o" changes to a "ue.") Memorize them and then see the tables for their complete conjugations.

Tener – to have
Querer – to want
Poder – to be able to

tener:

Spanish	English
Yo **tengo**	I **have**
Tú **tienes**	You **have**
Él, Ella **tiene**	He/she **has**
Nosotros **tenemos**	We **have**
Ellos, Ellas **tienen**	They **have**

querer:

Spanish	English
Yo **quiero**	I **want**
Tú **quieres**	You **want**
Él, Ella **quiere**	He/she **wants**
Nosotros **queremos**	We **want**
Ellos, Ellas **quieren**	They **want**

poder:

Spanish	English
Yo **puedo**	I **can**
Tú **puedes**	You **can**
Él, Ella **puede**	He/she **can**
Nosotros **podemos**	We **can**
Ellos, Ellas **pueden**	They **can**

C. Querer

Many of the nouns you learned in the last chapter can be used with querer. See the sample conversation below.

EXAMPLE 1

Spanish	English
<u>Marta:</u> ¿Qué quieres?	<u>Marta:</u> What do you want?
<u>Juan:</u> Quiero café.	<u>Juan:</u> I want coffee.

D. Two More Verbs

As with irregular –er verbs, you must memorize the conjugations of all irregular –ir verbs. Below are two new –ir verbs for you to memorize.

Dormir – to sleep
Decir – to say/tell

dormir:

Spanish	English
Yo **duermo**	I **sleep**
Tú **duermes**	You **sleep**
Él, Ella **duerme**	He/she **sleeps**
Nosotros **dormimos**	We **sleep**
Ellos, Ellas **duermen**	They **sleep**

56

decir:

Spanish	English
Yo **digo**	I **say**
Tú **dices**	You **say**
Él, Ella **dice**	He/she **says**
Nosotros **decimos**	We **say**
Ellos, Ellas **dicen**	They **say**

Lesson 3

A. Using Infinitive Verbs

Today's lesson includes verbs you have already learned. Recall that an "infinitive" is just a fancy name for a verb that hasn't been conjugated. Therefore, **tener** and **ir** are in the infinitive form.

B. I Have to

By using tener, a verb you learned yesterday, plus what you now know about infinitive verbs, you can now tell someone what you have to do. First, use the appropriate conjugation of the verb tener. Since we're saying "**I have to**," we'll use **tengo**. Next, add the word "**que**." You now have "**tengo que**." Finally select a verb (and a noun if you wish) of something you have to do. Let's use "**dormir**," which means, "to sleep." You now have "**tengo que dormir**." (I have to sleep!) It's that simple – the verb after "**tengo que**" never has to be conjugated! See the example.

EXAMPLE 1

Spanish	English
Yo **tengo que** <u>dormir</u>.	I **have to** <u>sleep</u>.
Yo **tengo que** <u>tocar</u> la guitarra.	I **have to** <u>play</u> the guitar.
Yo **tengo que** <u>comer</u>.	I **have to** <u>eat</u>.

C. One More Use for Infinitives

Don't turn the page yet! There is one more use for infinitives. You may have already picked up on this concept, but in case you didn't, here is an explanation. Any verb, which comes **AFTER** a conjugated verb in the **same** sentence, should be left as an infinitive! For example, Let's say, "Pablo wants to eat a taco." Two verbs are needed, **querer** (to want) and **comer** (to eat). First, conjugate querer, then add comer, and finally add "**el taco**." We now have "**Pablo quiere comer un taco**." That's simple, right? See the example.

EXAMPLE 2

Spanish	English
Pablo **quiere** <u>comer</u> un taco.	Pablo **wants** <u>to eat</u> a taco.
Ella **quiere** <u>tocar</u> la guitarra.	She **wants** <u>to play</u> the guitar.
Yo **quiero** <u>dormir</u>.	I **want** <u>to sleep</u>.

Exercise 7.3

Practice translating the sentences below using what you have learned in this chapter

She wants to sleep. = Ella _____ dormir.

He has to eat. = _____ tiene _____ comer.

I want to read. = Yo _____ _____.

They have to work. = Ellos _____ que _____.

Chapter 8 – "El Restaurante y la Ciudad"

(The Restaurant and the City)

Lesson 1

A. The Restaurant

This lesson is all about going out to eat! Below are a few general restaurant terms you need to know.

el menú – menu
el camarero – waiter
la propina – tip (gratuity)
el buffet – the buffet

B. Different Foods

Below are several different foods common both here and abroad. You may be familiar with many of the Spanish words already. Because there are hundreds of different foods, I've only included six or fewer in each section below. When traveling in a Spanish–speaking country, it might be a good idea to carry around a pocket dictionary so that you can quickly look up additional food names!

los aperitivos (appetizers):
el queso – cheese
la tortilla – tortilla
la salsa – salsa
la ensalada – salad
la sopa – soup

los platos principales (main dishes):
el taco – taco
el burrito – burrito
el pescado – fish
el biftec – steak
el jamón – ham
el pollo – chicken

frutas y verduras (fruits and vegetables):
la banana – banana

la **manzana** – apple
las **papas** – potatoes
el **maíz** – corn
la **lechuga** – lettuce

bebidas (beverages):
la **leche** – milk
la **limonada** – lemonade
la **agua** – water
el **café** – coffee
el **té** – tea

los **postres** (desserts):
el **helado** – ice cream
el **chocolate** – chocolate

C. Ordering Food

When the waiter comes to your table he or she will ask what you would like to drink and then return later to ask which meal you have selected. Note that waiters will never use the **tú** form when taking your order, as that would be considered disrespectful. When you enter a restaurant, expect to be greeted in the **Ud.** form. See the sample questions below and the examples.

¿Qué quiere Ud. beber? – What would you like to drink?
Yo quiero _____. – I would like _____.

¿Qué quiere Ud. comer? – What would you like to eat?
Yo quiero _____. – I would like _____.

EXAMPLE 1

Spanish	English
el camarero: ¿Qué quiere Ud. beber?	el camarero: What do you want to drink?
Diego: Yo quiero una limonada, por favor.	Diego: I would like lemonade, please.
el camarero: Un momento.	el camarero: One moment.

61

EXAMPLE 2

Spanish	English
<u>el camarero</u>: ¿ Qué quiere Ud. comer?	<u>el camarero</u>: What do you want to eat?
<u>Roberto</u>: Yo quiero un biftec y maíz.	<u>Roberto</u>: I would like a steak and corn.
<u>el camarero</u>: ¡Bien, gracias!	<u>el camarero</u>: Good, thanks!

Chapter 8

Lesson 2

A. Traveling In The City

There are several ways of traveling within large cities. Below is a list of some popular modes of transportation. You'll be using the verb <u>ir</u> to tell others how you are traveling. Usually, you use "a" with the verb <u>ir</u>, but this situation is an exception. Always use "por" when describing how you are traveling. See the example below.

el metro – subway
el autobús – bus
el carro – car
el taxi – taxi

¿Cómo vas? – How are you going (traveling)?
Voy por _____. – I am going by _____.

EXAMPLE 1

Spanish	English
Emilia: ¿Cómo vas a la escuela?	Emilia: How are you going to school?
Raquel: Voy por metro.	Raquel: I am going by the subway.
Emilia: Yo voy por metro, también!	Emilia: I am going by the subway too!

B. Places To Go In the City

Now you know how to get around in the city, but where will you go? On the next page is a list of a few common places people visit in the city. Memorize the list; then see the example on the next page.

el cine – movie theater
el museo – museum
el parque – park
el teatro – theater
oficina de correos – post office
buzón – mail box

¿Adónde vas a ir? – Where are you going to go?
Voy a ir a _____. – I am going to go to _____.

EXAMPLE 2

Spanish	English
Enrique: ¿Adónde vas a ir?	Enrique: Where are you going?
Marcos: Voy a ir al parque.	Marcos: I am going to the park.
Enrique: Yo voy al teatro.	Enrique: I am going to the theater!

C. Places To Go In the City

Are you going to be traveling *por taxi*? You'll need to know how to tell the taxi driver where you'd like to go!

EXAMPLE 3

Spanish	English
Enrique: ¡Quiero ir al Hotel Bolívar!	Enrique: I would like to go to the Hotel Bolívar.
Conductor del taxi: No es problema, Señor.	Taxi driver: No problem, Sir.
Enrique: Gracias.	Enrique: Thanks.

Lesson 3

A. Asking for Directions

If you are planning a trip to a Spanish–speaking country, this section will be especially useful for you. Anytime you go somewhere new, you may need to ask for directions at some point. Below you will learn how to ask for and interpret directions.

¿Dónde está _____**?** – Where is _____?
Está _____. – It is _____.

a la izquierda – to the left
a la derecha – to the right
enfrente de – in front of
detrás de – behind
cerca de – next(near) to

B. Popular Locations

Below are a few locations that are commonly used when giving directions. Memorize these so that when someone says, "El museo está cerca del banco." you will know what **el banco** is! See the example.

el banco – bank
el hospital – hospital
el hotel – hotel
la tienda – store
la escuela – school
la iglesia – church

EXAMPLE 1

Spanish	English
Pablo: ¿Dónde está el museo?	Pablo: Where is the museum?
Elena: El museo está cerca del banco.	Elena: The museum is near the bank.
Pablo: ¡Gracias!	Pablo: Thank you!

Chapter 9 – "El Viaje y mi Casa" *(The Trip and my House)*

Lesson 1

A. Boats, Planes, and Trains

Boats, planes and trains are the most common ways of travel when going long distances. This lesson will cover all three methods of transportation. Below are a few vocabulary words for commercial transportation.

el tren – train
el avión – airplane
el barco – boat

tarde – late
a tiempo – on time
el viaje – trip
el boleto – ticket
la maleta – suitcase
el cinturón de seguridad – seat belt
no fumar – no smoking

B. Hacer (New Verb)

The new verb you will learn in this section is hacer. Roughly translated, hacer means "**to do,**" or "**to make.**" Hacer has many uses, some of which will be explored in the next lessons. Unfortunately, hacer is an irregular verb. Therefore you will have to memorize all of the conjugations. See the table on the next page for the complete conjugations.

Hacer – to do/make

Hacer:

Spanish	English
Yo **hago**	I **do/make**
Tú **haces**	You **do/make**
Él, Ella **hace**	He/she **does/makes**
Nosotros **hacemos**	We **do/make**
Ellos, Ellas **hacen**	They **do/make**

C. Packing your Suitcase

Now that you've learned a few vocabulary words and a new verb, let's take a trip! Before you can go anywhere, however, you have to pack your bags! The verb to use for this is, you guessed it, **hacer**. See the example.

EXAMPLE 1

Spanish	English
Felipe: ¿Haces la maleta?	Felipe: Are you packing the suitcase?
Josefina: Sí, voy a hacer la maleta.	Josefina: Yes, I am going to pack the suitcase.
Felipe: ¡Gracias!	Felipe: Thank you!

D. Taking a Trip

Now that your bags are packed, it's time to go on your trip! Hacer can also be used to express, "I am taking a trip." See the example.

EXAMPLE 2

Spanish	English
Antonia: ¿Vas a hacer un viaje?	Antonia: Are you going to take a trip?
Alicia: Sí, voy a ir a España.	Alicia: Yes, I am going to go to Spain.
Antonia: ¡Muy bien!	Antonia: Very good!

Chapter 9

Lesson 2

A. Family Members

In this lesson you will learn the names of several different family members. Memorize the vocabulary list below; then continue.

la familia – family
el padre – father
la madre – mother
el hijo – son
la hija – daughter
el hermano – brother
la hermana – sister
el abuelo – grandfather
la abuela – grandmother
el tío – uncle
la tía – aunt

el perro – dog
el gato – cat

B. Hay (New Verb)

The new verb in this lesson is the easiest verb yet! **Hay** only has one conjugation! See the pronunciation guide (p. 78) to learn how to correctly say this verb. Then see the example on the next page.

Hay – there is/there are

EXAMPLE 1

Spanish	English
Hay dos gatos.	**There are** two cats.
Hay un perro.	**There is** one dog.

C. How Many Family Members?

Hay can be used to tell how many family members you have. See the question below, then the example.

¿Cuántas personas hay en la familia? – How many people are in your family?

EXAMPLE 2

Spanish	English
Carlos: ¿Cuántas personas hay en la familia?	Carlo: How many people are in the (your) family?
Ernesto: Hay dos personas en la familia.	Ernesto: There are two people in the (my) family.

Exercise 9.2

Fill in the blanks below using *hay* and possessives.

1) Hay dos _____ (cats).

2) Hay muchas _____ (suitcases).

3) _____ dos personas en la familia.

4) _____ pocos libros.

Chapter 9

Lesson 3

A. Parts of the House

This section contains several vocabulary words, which are useful for identifying different rooms in your home. Memorize the list below.

el dormitorio – bedroom
la sala – living room
la cocina – kitchen
el comedor – dining room
el baño – bathroom

B. Possessives

Possessives are words which show who is in possession of something. **My** cat, **your** house, and **his** car are all examples of possessives. Spanish possessives are used just like those in English. As with adjectives, to make a possessive word plural, add an "s" to the end. Whenever you possess more than one item (cats or books for example) the possessive word should be plural. Note that **su** can also be used to express "**their**" as well as something that belongs to "**you all.**" Memorize the list of common possessives below and then see the example on the next page.

Singluar	Plural
Mi – My	**Mis** – My
Tu – Your	**Tus** – Your
Su – His/Her/Your (formal)	**Sus** – His/Her/Your (formal)
Nuestro(a) – Our	**Nuestros(as)** – Our

EXAMPLE 1

Spanish	English
Nuestro gato.	**Our** cat.
Nuestros gatos.	**Our** cats.
Nuestra tía	**Our** aunt.
Nuestras tías.	**Our** aunts.
Mi amigo.	**My** friend.
Mis amigos.	**My** friends.

C. Alternate Uses For Tener

Tener, to have, can be used to express many other things. Although in English you say "I am cold," in Spanish you say "I have cold." The same is true for expressing hunger. "I have hunger." Finally, tener can be used to express how old you are. Just say "**tengo __ años.**" Memorize the list below of things that can be expressed with tener. See the example.

> **tener calor** – to be hot
> **tener frío** – to be cold
> **tener hambre** – to be hungry
> **tener __ años.** – to be _____ years old.

EXAMPLE 2

Spanish	English
Tengo <u>frío</u>.	I **am** <u>cold</u>.
Tengo <u>calor</u>.	I **am** <u>hot</u>.
Tengo <u>hambre</u>.	I **am** <u>hungry</u>.
¿Cuántos <u>años</u> **tienes**?	How <u>old</u> **are** you?
Tengo <u>cinco años</u>.	I **am** <u>five years old</u>.

Exercise 9.3

Practice using possessives below.

1) Hay dos personas en _____ (my) familia.

2) _____ (our) casa.

3) _____ (your) perro.

4) _____ (their) libros.

Chapter 10 – "La Tienda y la Moneda" *(The Store and Money)*

Lesson 1
A. New Verb

In this lesson you will learn one new verb. Fortunately for you, this verb is regular. Remember that because this is a regular verb, it can be conjugated like any other regular –er verbs. The complete conjugations are also available in the table below.

vender – to sell

Vender:

Spanish	English
Yo **vendo**	I **sell**
Tú **vendes**	You **sell**
Él, Ella **vende**	He/she **sells**
Nosotros **vendemos**	We **sell**
Ellos, Ellas **venden**	They **sell**

B. Using Vender

You can use <u>vender</u> to ask a store clerk if the store sells a particular item. Use vocabulary words you have learned in previous chapters, the words provided below, or words from a pocket dictionary! Remenmber: always speak to someone you do not know in the Ud. form.

el cepillo de dientes – toothbrush
la estampilla – stamp
la tarjeta postal – postcard
el bloque del sol – sunscreen
el periódico – newspaper

EXAMPLE 1

Spanish	English
¿Vende Ud. las estampillas?	Do you sell stamps?
Sí, vendemos estampillas.	Yes, we sell stamps.

C. Specialty Stores

There are several different types of stores both here and abroad. Below is a list of a few common stores. Memorize the list below.

Because there is no accent mark in *farmacia*, stress is on *ma*.

el almacén – department store
la farmacia – pharmacy
la pastelería – confections store
la panadería – baked goods store
el supermercado – grocery store

D. Various Products

Below is a list of several products sold at the stores above. You'll be using the verb <u>comprar</u>, which you learned in lesson 6.2 in this exercise. Memorize the list below, then see the example.

el pan – bread
el pastel – pastry/confection
el cuaderno – notebook
el libro – book
la computatora – computer
el teléfono – telephone
la aspirina – asprin

EXAMPLE 2

Spanish	English
Yo **compro** la medicina en <u>la farmacia</u>.	I **buy** medicine at <u>the pharmacy</u>.
Ella **compra** el pan en <u>la panadería</u>.	She **buys** bread at <u>the bakery</u>.

Lesson 2

A. Clothes

Several common articles of clothing are listed below. Memorize the list, then continue.

la camisa – shirt
los pantalones – pants
la corbata – tie
los zapatos – shoes
el suéter – sweater
la chaqueta – jacket/coat

B. Asking a Store Clerk For Help

If you cannot find an item in a store, you may need to ask a clerk for help. With this example, you will ask for the location of a specific item using the verb <u>estar</u> (see chapter 4 for a review). You will also be using the "directions" vocabulary you learned in chapter 8. With what you know, you can also form your own questions. See the example.

¿Dónde está _____? – Where are _____?
Está _____. – There are _____.

EXAMPLE 1

Spanish	English
¿Dónde están las camisas?	Where are the shirts?
Están a la izquierda de los pantalones.	They are to the left of the pants.

C. One Last Verb

It's time for one final verb! <u>Gustar</u> is used to describe something that you like or enjoy. (Literally, it describes something that pleases you.) It is not conjugated like traditional verbs. Instead, you will only use two conjugations and object pronouns of which we will only work with three: me, te, and nos. Nouns or verbs can be added onto the end to express things such as "I enjoy sports," or "I enjoy eating." Use **gusta** for singular objects, and **gustan** for plural objects. For example, if the apple is pleasing to you – use **gusta**. If sports are pleasing to you – use **gustan**.

gusta – *it* pleases
gustan – *they* please

me – me
te – you
nos – we

EXAMPLE 2

Spanish	English
Me gustan los deportes.	**I like** sports. (Sports are pleasing to me.)
Te gusta el gato.	**You like** the cat. (The cat is pleasing to me.)
Nos gusta la biblioteca.	**We like** the library. (The library is pleasing to us.)
Me gusta comer.	**I like** to eat. (Eating is pleasing to me.)

Lesson 3

A. More Numbers

Below are numbers 100–1000. Notice that "cientos" is the second part of each number below (from 200–900). Memorize the list below; then continue.

cien(to) – 100
doscientos – 200
trescientos – 300
cuatrocientos – 400
quinientos – 500
seiscientos – 600
setecientos – 700
ochocientos – 800
novecientos – 900
mil – 1,000

Using these numbers is just like using double–digit numbers. There is only one "**y**," which goes before the 1's place. The **y** <u>only</u> goes between the 10's place and 1's place. We'll practice writing **334**. Remember that to form **34** you take, "**treinta**," add, "**y cuatro**," and end up with "**treinta y cuatro**." Now just add that to "**trescientos**." You now have, "**trescientos treinta y cuatro**." That's it!

B. How Much Is This?

Occasionally items in stores don't have price tags. You may need to ask a store clerk how much something costs. See the example on the next page.

¿Cuánto es? – How much is this?
Es _____. – It is _____.

EXAMPLE 1

Spanish	English
¿**Cuánto es** <u>la corbata</u>?	**How much is** <u>the tie</u>?
Es <u>diez pesos</u>.	**It is** <u>ten pesos</u>.

C. Paying For Items

There are several different currencies you may use if you visit a Spanish–speaking country. Remember to check the exchange rates in foreign countries before making a purchase. See the list below for examples of a few different types of currency.

el dinero – money
la moneda – coins
en efectivo – cash
la tarjeta de crédito – credit card

el euro – used throughout Europe
el peso – used in Mexico
la peseta – used in Spain

EXAMPLE 2

Spanish	English
¿Puedo pagar con tarjeta de crédito?	Can I pay with a credit card?
Sí, Ud. puede pagar con tarjeta de crédito.	Yes, you can pay with a credit card.

Exercise 10.3

Translate the numbers below.

1) Doscientos treinta y cuatro.

_____

2) Five hundred thirty-two.

_____

3) Seven hundred five.

_____

4) One hundred ninety-one.

_____

5) Quinientos quince.

_____

Congratulations!

¡MUY BIEN! You have successfully completed Dive Into Spanish, Level 1. Now you will be able to converse with Spanish speakers everywhere! What you have learned within this book, in this short amount of time, is enough to equip you for an overseas vacation, or further study. I hope you feel that you've learned a lot and enjoyed yourself in the process.

Of course there is more to Spanish than what you have learned here. You will never be able to learn the entire Spanish language. Then again, you will never learn the entire English language! However, you now have a great foundation to build on, should you choose to continue your Spanish studies! Additionally, Italian, French, German, Portuguese and Latin are all in the same family as Spanish. You may find that these languages are now easier to learn!

¡Buena Suerte! (Good Luck!)
Chris Green

Acknowledgements

Thank you to Professor Marilyn Walker of Emory & Henry College for spending many, many hours advising me in the writing and editing of this book (and for putting up with me!). I couldn't have asked for a better Spanish expert to help me make this book a reality!

Thank you to Purdue University's "Foreign/Second Language Instruction Clip Art Collection" project for graciously allowing me to use many of their excellent clip art images in this book.

Last, but not least, thank you to each Spanish teacher and professor I have ever had. This book would not have been possible without you all.

Spanish Q&A

This section will answer many common questions you may have about Spanish.

- Why are the words, "**yo, él**, and **ella**," sometimes left out of example sentences?

  Using these pronouns is not always absolutely necessary. Each verb conjugation is different in Spanish, unlike English, therefore eliminating the need to always use these pronouns. So you can say, "Leo un libro," or, "Yo leo un libro." Either is correct.

- Is there a difference between the Spanish spoken in South America and Spain?

  Naturally, due to geographical differences, there are variations in dialects of this language. However, most of these are not significant enough to make a big difference in communication. In comparison, someone from South America conversing with someone from Spain is similar to someone from the United States talking to someone from Great Britain. Most of the words and phrases in this book can be used broadly – across Spain and South America.

- What about vosotros?

  Vosotros is not used except in Spain and in often older literature (such as the King James Version of the Bible). For this reason, the vosotros conjugations of verbs are not taught in Dive Into Spanish, Level 1.

- What about the past (preterit, imperfect) and future tenses?

  Tenses such as the preterit, imperfect and Future are beyond the scope of this book. You can learn these tenses from a more advanced book, or by taking Spanish classes in a college or university.

- Are accent marks important?

  No. Accent marks are vital. The purpose of accent marks is to alert you when to emphasize a vowel in a word. Some words can have completely different meanings if the accents are left out. If you forget and leave out an accent, though, you will likely still be understood. See "Getting Started" for more on accents.

Spanish Q&A (cont.)

- How can I learn more Spanish?

    You can learn more Spanish by reading Spanish magazines, watching Spanish TV or movies or taking Spanish classes in a college or university.

Glossary

This glossary includes all vocabulary words in this book. Although a few additional words have been added, this should not be considered a complete dictionary. For your convenience, verbs have been marked.

– A –

abril – april.
abburido – bored.
la abuela – grandmother.
el abuelo – grandfather.
adiós – goodbye.
agua – water.
agosto – august.
alto – tall.
amarillo – yellow.
el amigo– friend.
anaranjado– orange.
años – years.
antes de – before.
antipatico – not nice.
los aperitivos – appetizers.
a tiempo – on time.
el autobús – bus.
a veces – sometimes.
el avion – plane.
azul – blue.

– B –

la banana – banana.
la banca – bank.
el baño – bathroom.
bajo – short.
la barca – boat.
beber (v.) – to drink.
las bebidas – drinks.
la biblioteca – library.
la bicicleta – bicycle.
bien – good.
el biftec – steak.

el billette – ticket.

blanco – white.

buenos días – good morning.

buenos noches – good evening.

buenos tardes – good afternoon.

el buffet – buffet.

el burrito – burrito.

– C –

el café – coffee.

el camareron – waiter.

calor – hot.

la camisa – shirt.

el carro – car.

catorce – 14.

cero – 0.

la chaqueta – jacket/coat.

ciao – goodbye.

el chocolate – chocolate.

ciento – 100.

cinco – 5.

cincuenta – 50.

el cine – movie theater.

cinturón de seguridad – seat belt.

la cocina – kitchen.

cómo – how.

el comedor – dining room.

comer (v.) – to eat.

comprar (v.) – to buy.

la computadora – computer.

con – with.

la corbata – tie.

el cuaderno – notebook.

¿cuándo? – when.

¿cuánto? – how much.

cuarenta – 40.

cuatro – 4.

cuatrocientos – 400.

– D –

dar (v.) – to give.
de – of/from.
decir (v.) – to say.
despues de – after.
diciembre – December.
diecinueve – 19.
dieciocho – 18.
dieciséis – 16.
diecisiete – 17.
diez – 10.
el dinero – money.
divertido – fun.
doce – 12.
domingo – Sunday.
¿dónde? – where.
dormir (v.) – to sleep.
el dormitorio – bedroom.
dos – two.
doscientos – 200.
las drogas – medicine.

– E –

el – the.
Él – he.
Ella – she.
en – in.
enero – january.
enfermo – sick.
la ensalada – salad.
escribir (v.) – to write.
la escuela – school.
Español – Spanish.
estar (v.) – to be.
estupido – stupid.
el euro – money; used in Europe.

– F –

la familia – family.
la farmacía – pharmacy.

febrero – february
frio – cold.
las fruitas – fruits.
fumar (v.) – to smoke.

– G –

el gato – cat.
gracias – thanks.
los grandes almacenes – department store.
la guitarra – guitar.

– H –

hablar (v.) – to talk.
hacer (v.) – to do/make.
hambre – hungry.
hasta luego – see you later.
hasta mañana – see you tomorrow.
hasta pronto – see you soon.
hay (v.) – there is/there are.
el helado – ice cream.
la hermana – sister.
el hermano – brother.
la hija – daughter.
el hijo – son.
hola – hello.
el hospital – hospital.
el hotel – hotel.
hoy – today.

– I –

la iglesia – church.
inglés – English.
inteligente – intelligent.
ir (v.) – to go.

– J –

el jamon – ham.
jueves – Thursday.
julio – July.

junio – June.

– L –

la – the (fem.).
el libro – book.
las – the (fem, plural).
la leche – milk.
la lechuga – lettuce.
leer (v.) – to read.
la limonada – lemonade.
llegar (v.) – to arrive.
los – the (mas, plural).
lunes – Monday.

– M –

el maíz – corn.
la madre – mother.
la maleta – suitcase.
malo – bad.
mañana – tomorrow.
la manzana – apple.
marrón – brown.
martes – Tuesday.
marzo – march.
mayo – may.
el menú – menu.
el metro – subway.
mi – my.
miércoles – Wednesday.
mil – 1,000.
mirar (v.) – to look.
la moneda – coins.
moreno – dark (complexion/hair).
mucho – much.
el museo – museum.
muy – very.
muy bien – very good.
muy mal – very bad.

– N –

nada – nothing.

nadar (v.) – to swim.

necesitar (v.) – to need.

negro – black.

no – no.

noche – night.

nosotros – we.

novecientos – 900.

noventa – 90.

noviembre – November.

nueve – 9.

nuestro – our.

– O –

ochenta – 80.

ocho – 8.

ochocientos – 800.

octubre – October.

once – 11.

– P –

la padre – father.

el pan – bread.

la panadería – bakery.

los pantalones – pants.

las papas – potatoes.

el parque – park.

el pastel – pastry/confection.

la pastelería – confections store.

el periódico – newspaper

el perro – dog.

el pescado – fish.

la peseta – peseta, used primarily in Spain.

el peso – peso, used primarily in Mexico.

el piano – piano.

pie – on foot (walking).

los platos principales – main dishes.

poder (v.) – to be able to.

¿por qué? – why.

los postres – deserts.
la propina – gratuity.

– Q –

¿qué? – what.
querer (v.) – to want.
el queso – cheese.
¿quién? – who.
quince – 15.
quinientos – 500.

– R –

el restaurante – restaurant.
rojo – red.
rubio – blonde.

– S –

sábado – Saturday.
la sala – living room.
el salsa – salsa.
seiscientos – 600.
señor, Sr. – Mr.
señora, Sra. – Mrs.
señorita, Srta.. – Miss
septiembre – September.
ser (v.) – to be.
serio – serious.
seis – 6.
sesenta – 60.
setecientos – 700.
setenta – 70.
siete – 7.
simpático – nice.
la sopa – soup.
su – his/her/your/their (formal)
el supermercado – supermarket.
el suéter – sweater.

– T –

el taco – taco.

tarde – afternoon.

tarde – late.

el taxi – taxi.

el té – tea.

el teatro – theatre.

el teléfono – telephone.

la televisión – television.

tener – to have.

la tienda – store.

la tía – aunt.

el tío – uncle.

tocar (v.) – to play (an instrument).

todos los días – every day.

tomar (v.) – to take.

la tortilla – tortilla.

trabajar (v.) – to work.

trece – 13.

el tren – train.

tres – 3.

trescientos – 300.

treinta – 30.

triste - sad

tu – your.

tú – you.

– U –

un – a (mas.).

una – a (fem.).

uno – 1.

usted, Ud. – you (formal).

ustedes, Uds. – you all (formal).

– V –

veinte – 20.

vender (v.) – to sell.

verde – green.

las verduras – vegetables.

el viaje – trip.
viernes – Friday.
violeta – purple.
vivir (v.) – to live.

– Y –
y – and.
yo – I.

– Z –
los zapatos – shoes.

Answers to Exercises

1.1
Juan: Buenos **días**, Felipe, ¿ Qué **tal**?
Felipe: Muy bien, gracias, ¿y **tú**?
Juan: Muy bien.
Felipe: Bien. Ciao.
Juan: ¡Hasta **luego**!

1.2
el carro (the car).
el taco (a taco)
la tienda (the store).
la maleta (a suitcase).
la manzana (the apple).

1.3
Twenty–one **veintiuno**.
Veintinueve **twenty-nine**.
Twenty–two **veintidos**.
Veintiocho **twenty-eight**.
Twenty–five **veinticinco**.
Veintitrés **twenty-three**.

2.1
Yo **soy** Elena.
Ella **es** una chica.
Él **es** Roberto.
Tú **eres** Maricarmen.

2.2 #1
Marta: Hola, ¿**Quién** eres?
Carlos: **Soy** Carlos.
Marta: Hola, Carlos. Mucho **gusto**.
Carlos: El **gusto** es **mío**. ¿Quién es ella?
Marta: Ella **es** Maricarmen.
Carlos: Hola, Maricarmen. ¡**Mucho** gusto!

2.2 #2

<u>Marcos</u>: Hola, ¿Quién **es** Ud.?
<u>Maria</u>: Yo **soy** Maria. ¿y Quién es **Ud.**?
<u>Marcos</u>: **Yo** soy Marcos. ¡Mucho **gusto**!

2.3

1) ¿Cómo eres?
Yo soy **(your name)**.

2) ¿**De** dónde eres?
Yo **soy** de los Estados Unidos.

3) ¿De dónde **es** él?
Él es de España.

4) ¿Cómo es **ella**?
Ella es **rubia** (blonde) y **simpatica** (nice).

5) ¿Eres **morena**?
Sí, yo **soy** morena.

3.1

los bolígrafos (the pens).
los libros (some books).
las escuelas (some schools).
las casas (the houses).
las papas (some potatoes).

3.3 #1

Forty–three **cuarenta y tres**.
Sixty–seven **sesenta y siete**.
Fifty–one **cincuenta y uno**.
Eighty–two **ochenta y dos**.
Twenty–five **veinticinco**.
One hundred thirty–one **ciento treinta y uno**.

3.3 #2

1) May 6.
Hoy es el seis de mayo.

2) 3:30 P.M.
Son las tres y media de la tarde.

3) June 5.
Hoy es el cinco de junio.

4) 5:15 A.M.
Son las cinco y cuarto de la mañana.

4.2
Raul: Hola, Daniela. ¿Dónde está Maricarmen?
Daniela: Maricarmen **está** en la biblioteca.
Raul: Ah. ¿**Dónde** están los estudiantes?
Daniela: Jajaja! Los estudiantes **están** en la escuela.

4.3
Emilia: Hola, Pablo. ¿**Cómo** estás?
Pablo: Estoy **bien**, ¿y tú?
Emilia: Bien, **gracias**.
Pablo: ¿y Marco? ¿Cómo **está** él?
Emilia: Él **está** bien.

5.2
Ella va a ir **al** banco.
Nosotros somos **del** Brazil.
Yo voy **a la** escuela.
Elena **va** a **la** tienda.
Tú eres **de** los Estados Unidos.

5.3
Vamos **por** el carro.
Voy **a** pie.
Voy a **nadar** (swim).
Ella va a **ir** a la biblioteca.

6.1
- ¿**Qué** miras?
- **Miro** los deportes, ¿y tú?

- Miro **los deportes**, también.

- Hablas inglés?
- No, no hablo **inglés**. **Hablo** español y alemán.

6.2
- ¿**Qué** necesitas?
- **Necesito** una estampilla.

- ¿**Dónde** trabajas?
- **Trabajo** en un restaurante.

7.3
She wants to sleep. = Ella **quiere** dormir.
He has to eat. = **Él** tiene **que** comer.
I want to read. = Yo **quiero leer**.
They have to work. = Ellos **tienen** que **trabajar**.

9.2
1) Hay dos **gatos** (cats).
2) Hay muchas **maletas** (suitcases).
3) **Hay** dos personas en la familia.
4) **Hay** pocos libros.

9.3
1) Hay dos personas en **mi** (my) family.
2) **Nuestra** (our) casa.
3) **Tu** (your) perro.
4) **Sus** (their) libros.

10.3
1) Doscientos treinta y cuatro.
Two hundred thirty five.

2) Five hundred and thirty-two.
Quinientos treinta y dos.

3) Seven hundred five.
Setecientos cinco.

4) One hundred ninety-one.
Cientos noventa y uno.

5) Quinientos quince.
Five hundred fifteen.

www.ingramcontent.com/pod-product-compliance
Lightning Source LLC
Chambersburg PA
CBHW021208020426
42331CB00003B/256